Moira McQueen

Walking Together

A PRIMER ON THE NEW SYNODALITY

TWENTY-THIRD
PUBLICATIONS

NOVALIS

© 2022 Novalis Publishing Inc.

Cover design: Martin Gould
Cover image: Getty Images
Layout: Audrey Wells

Published by Novalis

Publishing Office
1 Eglinton Avenue East, Suite 800
Toronto, Ontario, Canada
M4P 3A1

Head Office
4475 Frontenac Street
Montréal, Québec, Canada
H2H 2S2

en.novalis.ca

Cataloguing in Publication is available from Library and Archives Canada
ISBN: 978-2-89830-037-0

Printed in Canada.

Published in the United States by
Twenty-Third Publications
One Montauk Avenue
New London, CT 06320
(860) 437-3012 or (800) 321-0411
www.twentythirdpublications.com
ISBN: 978-1-62785-692-8

We acknowledge the support of the Government of Canada.

5 4 3 2 1   26   25   24   23   22

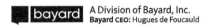 A Division of Bayard, Inc.
Bayard CEO: Hugues de Foucauld

Contents

Introduction

I n the chapter I wrote for *Looking to the Laity*, recently published by Novalis, I ended with these words about the laity's role in shaping the future Church: "A diocesan, regional or local synod could be a reasonable strategy for lay people to have a place in the Church, for their voice to be heard in dialogue with official Church leaders.... What a way forward that would be for our future Church!"[1]

Not only would this be a "reasonable" way, but Pope Francis sees synodality as necessary for Church leaders and laity to "walk together" in a different way that allows the contributions of both, as befits their common baptism as members of the People of God in shaping the future Church. This vision reflects the spirit and intent of the Second Vatican Council, which, in *Lumen Gentium* in particular, emphasized our common baptism as the essential qualification for membership in the Body of Christ, in which each one of us has a specific vocation and purpose. This radical equality conferred by baptism needs to be recalled and revitalized in every aspect of Church life until it is more adequately realized by all, especially among the laity. This primer suggests that one way to do so is to become familiar with and to embrace the emerging development of synodality – walking together – on a local and global basis.

What *is* synodality?

The word "synodality" is beginning to appear everywhere, and to some people it seems to be coming out of the blue. The fact that the Synod of Bishops taking place in 2023 is *about* synodality tells us that here is something that the whole Church is being asked to address.

Although it may sound like a strange word to Catholic ears, it is not a new concept. The word itself needs some explanation. The Second Vatican Council used the terms "council" and "synod" somewhat interchangeably to describe its own proceedings, although "council" was used more often and is more familiar to us. The two words, however, have the same meaning: one title deriving from Latin (*con*) and the other from Greek (*syn*) meaning "together with," and the Greek *hodos*, meaning "way." *Lumen Gentium*, the Council's Dogmatic Constitution on the Church, established the concept of Church as the whole "People of God" before moving into considerations of hierarchy and laity.

> *Walking together is a way for lay people to further their baptismal mission through joining the ordained in the discernment gifted by the Spirit to all the baptized, with the difference that now, working together, there is the intention that their voice will be heard more proportionately in the Church as it continues on the Way.*

Vatican II and synodality

A major thrust of the Second Vatican Council is that the *whole* People of God is now the emphasis: a communion, a joint membership of every individual by virtue of the sacrament of baptism. Although the fledgling Church of Jesus Christ had been more of a communion at its beginning – they all shared in common what they owned, although there was leadership – there is no doubt that the gap between hierarchy and laity became quite wide very early on. The Council Fathers recognized that and sought to restore the concept of the "whole" Church – the Body of Christ of which we are all members, equal in personal dignity albeit with varieties of gifts and vocations as the Spirit wills.

Another major result of the Council's vision of the whole People of God walking together on the Way was Pope Paul VI's re-establishment of the Synod of Bishops. This terminology was used to distinguish it from the word "council" itself, which includes all the bishops, whereas the synod was to be a representative body, with a certain number of bishops representing their countries. It was to meet regularly, providing an opportunity to meet more frequently to discuss various topics. There had been a gap of almost a century between the First and Second Vatican Councils, for example, and the world had changed in multiple ways in that period. Pope Paul, in response to the Council, reintroduced synodal practice into the Catholic world, although other denominations, notably the Anglican and Orthodox communions, had maintained this way of consulting their members over the centuries.

The Council's emphasis on the whole Church as the People of God lessens the perceived distinction between clerics and lay, hierarchy and "lower-archy," pastors and their "flock." Informed by *Lumen Gentium*, the theological and pastoral aspects of walking together gradually developed.

The purpose of this primer is to

* describe those aspects,
* situate them in their current expression and
* describe how they are being revitalized and applied at the Vatican itself and in the Catholic world.

Many Catholics are aware that there have been several synods since Vatican II (1962–65), and several well-publicized synods have been held during Francis's papacy. The Synod on the Amazon garnered worldwide attention, as had his encyclical *Laudato Si'*, but previous popes also recognized synods as a means to implement more fully the Council's vision that the whole People is needed for the Church's mission of evangelization. Not only that, but within their respective vocational roles, each of the baptized has a part to play in the discernment needed to envision the path for the whole Church, meaning clergy and laity should walk and work *together*.

Synodality: Pope Francis's focus

Pope Francis has consolidated Church teaching on synodality, added to it and given it a much sharper focus. It is not just *a* way for the People of God: he calls it *the* way. He has emphasized that synodality is "an essential dimension of the Church." If that is true, we should be able to see that there is something already present in the Church signified by the term "synodality," something important that has been there since the beginning.

This is a foundational point in the writing of this primer: that this is not truly a new concept, but an old one with new elements. The idea of everyone in the Church walking together has been there since the beginning, although now the *way* of walking is different.

Pope Francis means to make the process of being a synodal Church more systematic, and so he has instituted a Secretariat of the Synod to implement his vision and make it a reality by helping dioceses and conferences of bishops to see how this can be done. His teaching invites us to understand that synodality is essential in the way we experience membership in the Church today and is the way for shaping its direction in the future. At the same time, he invites us to understand that this is the way intended for the Church from its beginning.

Several modern developments highlight the existence of a sort of synodality from a more secular viewpoint: that is, "Nothing about us without us!" They appeal to those who want to participate in politics, in policies and in governance, demanding to have their voices heard. This desire finds expression in all sorts of social and political movements and, while we are sometimes reminded that the Church is not a democracy, neither need it be seen as *only* hierarchical. Another result of the Second Vatican Council that is still gradually developing is increased lay participation in the higher echelons of the Church. The acceptance of the importance of synodality encourages further steps in that direction: for example, the promotion of women to several Vatican offices, which had been unthinkable before.

What lies ahead?

Will there be resistance? More than likely. Some people might perceive this way of proceeding as a threat to the clerical "establishment" and to the usual way of doing business, even spiritual business. For those with a different vision, this conversation is happening at an opportune time, since, even before the COVID-19 pandemic, the laity were looking for deeper layers of involvement and responsibility. In that light, it seems equally essential that both clergy and lay people become knowledgeable about walking together as a way forward in determining what is best for the Church.

This primer will present the view that synodality, walking together, is a way for lay people to further their baptismal mission through joining the ordained in the discernment gifted by the Spirit to all the baptized, with the difference that now, working together, there is the intention that their voice will be heard more proportionately in the Church as it continues on the Way.

"It is precisely this path of synodality which God expects of the Church of the third millennium."—Spoken at a ceremony commemorating the 50th anniversary of the Institution of the Synod of Bishops, 2015

To walk together is the constitutive way of the Church; the figure that enables us to interpret reality with the eyes and heart of God; the condition for following the Lord Jesus and being servants of life in this wounded time. The breath and pace of the Synod show what we are, and the dynamism of communion that animates our decisions; only in this way can we truly renew our pastoral ministry and adapt it to the mission of the Church in today's world; only in this way can we address the complexity of this time, thankful for the journey accomplished thus far, and determined to continue it with *parrhesia.—Pope Francis, at the opening of the 70th General Assembly of the Italian Episcopal Conference, 2017*

Reflection questions

1. Are you familiar with the term "synodality"? What does it mean to you?

2. Have you heard much locally about Synods of Bishops over the years? What do you remember about these events?

3. Can you think of ways in which clergy and laity can walk together for the good of the Church?

1

A Brief History of Councils and Synods in the Roman Catholic Tradition

Scriptural foundations of synodality

From a scriptural basis, the concept of synodality begins with what is often named the Council of Jerusalem. We read about this in Acts of the Apostles, chapter 15, where we learn that from the very beginning, the Apostles and their early followers worked together in discerning how their new Way, really the way outlined by Jesus Christ, was to be followed. They had been raised in the Jewish tradition, but other disciples and followers, non-Jews, were increasing in numbers. The formal structure of the Catholic Church that is so familiar to us today and that has continued down through the centuries was then in its embryonic Christian form. It certainly did not bear the name "the Catholic Church"!

Just as today there are different views of how to organize, evangelize and worship, so then, too, there were factions and strong personalities at play. Yet, when we read the book of Acts and look at how the Apostles and their disciples approached these matters, we can see how willing they were to be guided by the Spirit after experiencing the events of Pentecost and how they strove to follow the Way that Jesus had shown them by listening to the Spirit.

A picture emerges as, almost inevitably, differences began to appear between Jewish Christians and newly baptized Gentiles. The Apostles and Jesus were Jewish, of course, and perhaps had been originally of different persuasions (such as Pharisee or Sadducee); recognizing Jesus as the Messiah involved a radical change in their Jewishness, which did not simply disintegrate or fade away. Their religious practices of circumcision, temple offerings, the Law of Moses and so on collided with the different religious and spiritual experiences and practices of Gentiles, although now transcended by their common baptism in the name of Jesus the Christ. It was not surprising that Gentiles refused to be circumcized and to follow the Mosaic law, as they were formed in their own religious traditions. Questions, even disputes, inevitably arose. According to the Vatican website, an issue about the circumcision of non-Jews arose around 48 AD, when some Christians coming from Judea resisted the procedure in the name of their Christian freedom. Paul and Barnabas agreed that this rite should not be imposed on them; the community in Antioch decided to consult the Apostles and elders in Jerusalem. The assembly gathered there discerned the missionary leadership of Peter for the circumcised and of Paul for the uncircumcised.[2]

What we see happening here is almost like the first general meeting of the followers of the Way, as their new group was called, meeting at their "head office" in Jerusalem, where most of the Apostles remained. In relating this major conflict that had arisen, Acts 16 contains these words: "It has seemed good to the Holy Spirit and to us..." (16:28). Right from the start, therefore, their meeting was convened in the name of the Spirit, the giver of wisdom, peace and all the other gifts. Given that the meeting occurred so soon after Pentecost, the Apostles were most likely still on fire with the spiritual gifts bestowed on them, fuelling their courage, authority, sense of purpose and determination to follow the Lord Jesus, who had gone to his Father, sending them the Spirit as their guide, as he had promised.

Biblical scholar Jaroslav Pelikan writes of this episode:

> This entire chapter has served throughout Christian history as a model for decision-making in the church, and as a charter both for authority at church councils and for the authority of church councils. Therefore, these very words, "it has seemed good to the Holy Spirit and to us," identifying the voice of a council with the voice and will of the Holy Spirit and not "something human," were quoted by later councils and confessions, including some Protestant ones.[3]

In terms of leadership at the Council of Jerusalem, Pelikan points out that many of us would have assumed that Peter was the leader, already in a sense recognized as the "first Pope," the automatic leader from the beginning. Matthew's Gospel proclaimed Peter as the "rock" on which Christ promised to build a church, against which the gates of hell would not prevail (Matt. 16:18). While Peter's is the first name to appear in this part of the Scripture, Pelikan carefully reminds us that it was "as a prominent participant among other participants, not as a monarch or even, for now, as *primus inter pares*"[4] (first among equals), which is how the papacy is still regarded today.

It is the Apostle James, not Peter, who exclaims, "My brothers, listen to me," and announces his judgment on the matter of circumcision: "we should not trouble those Gentiles who are turning to God" (Acts 15:13, 19). Earlier in the chapter we read: "The apostles and the elders met together to consider this matter" (15:6), revealing that they had gathered and were working together, in the Spirit. Chapter 16 confirms this, describing "the decisions that had been reached by the apostles and elders who were in Jerusalem" (16:4). Pelikan emphasizes the statement that the decisions were made "by all of them in concert together, neither by James alone nor by

Peter alone."[5] These decisions, according to Acts 16:4, carried the weight of rules to be followed by all. This was an all-important foundation for the evolution of ways to handle questions and disputes. It also raised questions of leadership, participation and authority, questions that are still being considered today. This is a well-documented incident from the early Church that relies on the Spirit and communal discernment. In many ways, it seems surprisingly modern and inclusive, and indeed modern synods are intended to take place in that vein.

Synodal meetings in the early Church

Although divisions happen, as perhaps they will over the implications of synodality, the guidance of the Spirit, prayerfully invoked, will always steer the Church toward truth and the right way, no matter how long that may take.

Further examples of this Christian way of walking together appear in the following centuries as councils and synods continued to be held, such as the Council of Nicea in 325 AD, which clarified the basic tenets of the institution based on Christ as "one, holy, catholic and apostolic." These are the hallmarks of the Church we know today as "Catholic" and of its guaranteed succession from Christ's original Apostles. When we recite the Apostles' Creed or the Nicene Creed, we can look back over the centuries and see the Spirit at work through synodality in shaping "the way" according to the Word. It is astonishing that we take our creeds and their history for granted without questioning the human processes that shaped them, guided by the Spirit, but we tend to do so.

Later synods dealt with such important topics as the two natures in the one person of Christ, the relationship of the Father and Son with the Holy Spirit, and other fundamental points of Christian theology, all of which were controversial and potentially divisive. They were, however, resolved. That is a helpful reminder for our own times: although divisions happen, as perhaps they will over the implications of synodality, the guidance of the Spirit, prayerfully invoked, will always steer the Church toward truth and the right way, no matter how long that may take.

Synodality in other Christian churches

Although the number of major synods declined over the years, the synodal path was continued in the Eastern Church after the schism with the West in 1054, while the Eastern Catholic Church continued to hold synod gatherings for important decision making, as has the Anglican Church since its inception. There were, of course, some famous synods in the United Kingdom long before the Anglican Church was established, perhaps the most famous being the Synod of Whitby in 664. It settled the date on which Easter was to be celebrated, there being differences between the Church overseen by Irish monks evangelizing from St Columba's monastery in Iona and those following the decision of the Roman Church, in turn looking at a method from Alexandria. Delegates from these countries were present, attesting to the international composition of synods in their earliest days and demonstrating the reach of the Church and its seal of being "Catholic."

Modern communications and the synodal process

The history of synods and councils in Christian churches is important for our understanding of doctrinal changes or added nuances, as well as being important for gathering church leaders to discuss new developments and disputed questions. Although communications are much easier these days, historically the exchange of letters and missives from Rome and other dioceses and countries could take months, and bishops from far-flung places would have little opportunity to meet together. It must have been even harder to settle disputes or to know what other people were thinking or doing about certain matters. These days, a message flashed on a screen can engender responses or commentary within hours or even minutes!

Catholicism and synodality after the Reformation

In general, in the Roman Catholic Church, coming together in synods and councils dwindled almost completely after the Reformation in the 16th century, but not before the famous Council of Trent took place between 1545 and 1563. The Christian world had changed dramatically, and the Roman Church now had to focus both on holding its ground and on reinforcing its doctrinal corpus. After a long hiatus and almost a century apart, the events of two Vatican Councils made a great impact on the way the Catholic Church envisioned itself. In particular, the Second Vatican Council led to a retrieval of the Synod of Bishops as a way of continuing the global, episcopal participation that the Council itself achieved. Regular meetings of bishops were judged necessary and, fortunately, more possible than ever before in the Church's history. (With today's technology, meetings can be held remotely as well.)

Reflection questions

1. Does the role of James at the Council of Jerusalem surprise you? Why or why not?

2. Reflect on the importance of the Holy Spirit for the Church. Where do you see the Spirit at work today?

3. Reflect on the role of early synods and the development of unity in the early Church. How do you see synods helping or hindering the work of today's Church?

2

Vatican II and
Lumen Gentium

The significance of the "People of God"

The Second Vatican Council document *Lumen Gentium* is
of major theological importance in the way it envisages the
Roman Catholic Church.[6] Wanting to move away from the
more sharply defined separation that had grown between priests
and people, the Council Fathers envisioned the Church as the whole
"People of God," worshipping and working together to evangelize
the world, each person with his or her own role to play. There is
no doubt that in many countries and cultures, this was a radical
change from a "hierarchy first, laity second" approach, where an
undesirable sense of superiority had crept in on the part of some
clergy and had been accepted or was unquestioned by many of the
laity. Whether stemming from a perceived superiority through
ordination, whereby the priest was seen as better and /or holier, or
out of respect for the priest's greater theological training, or from
local cultures that engendered an attitude that the priest could do
no wrong, the aura of difference around the priesthood was rarely
critiqued or seriously challenged. This led to a greater separation
between priest and people as well as to a diminished or lack of
recognition of lay gifts, charisms, skills and talents.

The discussions and theological contributions at the Council about this separation are an extensive study in themselves, and it is humbling to read the Council's internal critique of its own attitudes, culminating in the realization that it needed to reorient itself in this area. Many of the Council documents reflect this shift in the way they retrieve and re-emphasize the significance of the Sacrament of Baptism. The dignity and worth of every person, and our radical equality as creatures made by and in the image of God, reinforced the insight of *Lumen Gentium* that all the baptized together, without separation, form the People of God.

Even before Vatican II, widespread education had helped to shape lay people in ways formerly unknown, and an educated laity had posed a different set of questions about their role in the Church. Add to this the growth of democracy, the rise of the labour movement from the late 19th century on, the political tides against aristocracies, and the development of human rights and legal notions of equality, and it is understandable that many people started to think differently about their role and status in society. The Church, too, was part of this: witness Catholic social teaching that outlined the need for protecting working people and the common good proclaimed by Pope Leo XIII in encyclicals such as *Rerum Novarum* (1891), followed later by the social teachings of Pope John Paul II, a prominent contributor to proceedings at the Council. Social attitudes changed, and magisterial teaching began to reflect those changes, not least in its approach to the Catholic laity.

Lumen Gentium states that "the apostolate of the laity is a sharing in the church's saving mission" and acknowledges that "Through Baptism and Confirmation all are appointed to this apostolate by the Lord himself" (no. 33). Theologian Paul Lakeland emphasizes this point: that this mission "to make the church present and fruitful in those places and circumstances where it is only through them that it can become the salt of the earth [is] something that each lay person carries out on the authority of Christ, given in the sacraments of baptism and confirmation."[7] In the same section 33 of *Lumen Gentium*, the Council made a significant statement: "the laity can be called in different ways to more immediate cooperation in the apostolate of the hierarchy." Lakeland reminds us that at the time, the bishops were influenced by the good work done through groups such as Catholic Action. The bishops also noted that lay people "have, moreover, the capacity of being appointed by the hierarchy to some ecclesiastical offices with a view to a spiritual end" and could "share diligently in the salvific work of the Church according to their ability and the needs of the times." Further, *Lumen Gentium* says of the laity, which is again timely in light of synodality:

> to the extent of their knowledge, competence or authority the laity are entitled, and indeed sometimes duty-bound, to express their opinion on matters which concern the good of the church … this should be done through the institutions established by the church for that purpose … the laity should promptly accept in Christian obedience what is decided by the pastors … [who] should recognize and promote the dignity and responsibility of the laity … [and] willingly use their prudent advice and confidently assign offices to them in the service of the church, leaving them freedom and scope for activity. (no. 37)

Although to modern ears some of this may sound a little condescending, the Council took pains to redefine the clergy–laity relationship to a large extent, opening the door to the acceptance of lay contributions to and in the Church structure itself. This paved the way for new concepts of lay participation and even for the concept of synodality to re-emerge. One change builds on another…

Clarity on roles of bishops and pope

Pope Paul VI, who succeeded Pope John XXIII, was instrumental in formulating and contributing to many of the changes made by

> *The dignity and worth of every person, and our radical equality as creatures made by and in the image of God, reinforced the insight of* Lumen Gentium *that all the baptized together, without separation, form the People of God.*

the Council. Following this, the Council ratified *Christus Dominus* (Decree on the Pastoral Office of Bishops), stating in section 8 that the bishops, in their dioceses, have all the ordinary power needed to exercise their pastoral office. The Pope, however, can always reserve some cases for himself or others to adjudicate.

There had been some tension before the Council about the role of the papacy and the bishops. One theologian put it this way: "We can see that most of the Vatican II bishops from all over the world, whether they were part of the 'reformist' majority or of the 'conservative' minority, were convinced of the need for a new balance of powers between the papacy and the episcopacy, between the Roman Curia and the Episcopacy."[8] Massimo Faggioli notes that an emerging theme during Vatican II was the need for reform of the dicasteries of the Vatican central government, with several bishops proposing the creation of a new body within it, one that was more representative of them.[9]

A major concern raised by the bishops was the need for greater participation and consultation between the Pope and the bishops apart from the work of the Curia. The result was eventually the institution of the Synod of Bishops. This, too, was a retrieval of Church practice rather than a completely new idea, although some of the practical arrangements were very different from those in previous bodies. These synods could not comprise the whole Assembly of Bishops as Vatican II had done, but it was decided that a certain number of bishops would be elected from their home countries to represent their local Church.

This request and response account for the Council, reintroducing into the Roman Catholic Church what would develop into a broader concept of synodality, began at the Council through the establishment of a new Synod of Bishops. This was formally mandated by Pope Paul VI in September 1965 through his document *Apostolica Sollicitudo* (Apostolic Care), allowing more involvement of the bishops together with the Pope in matters concerning the Church. The retrieval of leaders in the Church "walking together" in this way not only redefined the working relationship between the Pope and the bishops as well as the bishops and the Curia, but also led to even wider consultation in the Church as lay people also began to be invited as participants, not just as observers.

Reflection questions

1. Reflect on our Church as the "People of God." What difference does this view of the Church make to us as members?

2. What differences still exist between clergy and lay people today, and why?

3. What do you think influenced the Council to "redefine" the Church?

3

Pope Francis
and Synodality

A round 20 Synods of Bishops had taken place from the time of the Second Vatican Council until the election of Pope Francis in 2013. They were mainly of two kinds: "ordinary" assemblies to consider matters of importance to the whole Church, and "special" gatherings dealing with more localized topics.

Pope Francis and synodality as a reality in Church practice at every level

In this chapter, Pope Francis's own words will be quoted several times, since from the beginning of his pontificate it was clear that he meant to develop more fully the structure of the Synod of Bishops and encourage synodality as a reality in Church practice at every level. There were early mentions of "walking together" in his speeches and writings; his interest in collaboration and consultation with the laity became evident. For example, in 2013, just a few months after he became Pope, statements such as the following started to appear in the Catholic press:

> [Francis] wants to change the way the universal Church is governed, in such a way that the local Church – dioceses, bishops' conferences – plays a much larger part in the decisions that affect it, while ensuring that Rome (the

Vatican, including his own Petrine ministry) better serves the Church worldwide. In short, Francis wishes to shorten the distance between Rome and the local Church, to ensure that they act better together.[10]

Although this was not about the laity specifically, the phrase "act better together" is another way of saying "act synodally," where the accent falls on *syn/together,* between Rome (the Curia) and the dioceses and, by extension, between dioceses and their members and/or between priests and parishioners.

Even before Francis became pope, Church leaders recognized that the structure and outcomes of synods were far from perfect. In 2004, Cardinal Schönborn of Vienna said that synods needed "more plenary discussion, more consultation on issues developing an atmosphere of a real debate, a real exchange, and to be liberated a little bit from that narrow framework that has developed in the last decades."[11] From his remarks, it is clear that the organization of synods left a lot to be desired, and it became increasingly clear that Pope Francis agreed with him.

During the Synod on Marriage and the Family in 2015, Pope Francis gave an outstanding address showing the seriousness of his conviction about the need for the synodal way throughout the Church. He said that from the beginning of his papacy, he wanted to bring the idea of synods to more prominence, as had been envisioned at Vatican II. After acknowledging the progress that had been made since the Council, he insisted:

> We must continue along this path. The world in which we live, and which we are called to love and serve, even with its contradictions, demands that the Church strengthen cooperation in all areas of her mission. It is precisely this path of *synodality* which God expects of the Church of the third millennium.[12]

The last sentence is interesting, even visionary: the Pope did not say that this is simply what *he* hoped for, but that *God* expects it of the current Church! In his first Apostolic Exhortation, *The Joy of the Gospel*, in 2013, Pope Francis noted that all the baptized can do the work of evangelization. This work should not be "carried out by professionals while the rest of the faithful would simply be passive recipients."[13]

He re-emphasized the important and somewhat overlooked concept of the *sensus fidei*, defined at the Second Vatican Council in *Lumen Gentium*:

> The entire body of the faithful, anointed as they are by the Holy One, cannot err in matters of belief. They manifest this special property by means of the whole peoples' supernatural discernment in matters of faith when "from the Bishops down to the last of the lay faithful" they show universal agreement in matters of faith and morals. That discernment in matters of faith is aroused and sustained by the Spirit of truth. It is exercised under the guidance of the sacred teaching authority, in faithful and respectful obedience to which the people of God accepts that which is not just the word of men but truly the word of God. (no. 12)

Lumen Gentium's teaching wanted to avoid the complete separation of the "teaching Church" (the Pope and the bishops) from the "learning Church" (the laity). In light of this principle, the laity has not only a "voice" but a voice that counts in matters of faith and morals.

Synodality and the *sensus fidei*

Being accountable to this *sensus fidei* is a hallmark of Pope Francis's pontificate. It was in consideration of this teaching that in 2014, before the Synod on Marriage and the Family, he requested that members of every diocese be consulted and asked to reply to a provided set of questions. This may not sound unusual in an era when surveys are commonplace, but it was the first time such a global consultation had taken place in the Catholic Church. The Pope's rationale was that, while the usual way of ascertaining the mind of the various dioceses on certain matters is still necessary,

> a consultation of this sort would never be sufficient to perceive the *sensus fidei*. But how could we speak about the family without engaging families themselves, listening to their joys and their hopes, their sorrows and their anguish?[14]

While such listening may sound obvious, it had never been done on such a scale. What took place in 2014 marked a major change in both theological and pastoral practice. Pope Francis underscored this, adding, "A synodal Church is a Church which listens, which realizes that listening 'is more than simply hearing'. It is a mutual listening in which everyone has something to learn."[15]

Significantly, the Pope quoted a maxim from the early Church: *Quod omnes tangit ab omnibus tractari debet* (What touches all must be discussed and approved by all), showing that there is rarely anything new under the sun in these matters. Today we might hear some groups call for "Nothing about us, without us!" but it's really the same pithy observation. Only after listening to the voice of the people should the synodal process continue through the work of the bishops, who "act as guardians, interpreters and witnesses of the faith of the whole Church, which they need to discern carefully from the changing currents of public opinion."[16]

The "listening" Church

Listening is the key, according to the Pope. He prayed to the Holy Spirit that the Synod Fathers be given the gift of listening, "to listen to God, so that with him we may hear the cry of his people; to listen to his people until we are in harmony with the will to which God calls us."[17] The synod process means first listening to the Bishop of Rome, but the Pope emphasized that this is not to be done "on the basis of his personal convictions but as the supreme witness to the *fides totius Ecclesiae* [the faith of the whole Church], 'the guarantor of the obedience and the conformity of the Church to the will of God, to the Gospel.'"[18]

Centuries earlier, Saint John Chrysostom said that "Church and Synod are synonymous"; the Pope pointed out that Jesus set Peter at the head of this new Church as the foundational "rock," responsible for converting people to this new Way.[19] Referring to the concept of Church as "People of God," the term found in *Lumen Gentium,* Pope Francis reminded his listeners that the structure of the Church is an inverted pyramid, where the base is at the top. As a result, he told the Assembly in 2015, "those who exercise authority are called 'ministers', because, in the original meaning of the word, they are the least of all." Underlining this concept even more strongly, he added, "the Successor of Peter is nothing else if not the *servus servorum Dei*" (the servant of the servers of God).[20] The whole People of God is addressed here, with the roles of laity, bishop and Pope clearly demarcated, but with a different emphasis. This is a Church that is to include the laity in a more definitive fashion and where those in authority are to remember they are called to serve, as must the Pope himself. Further, the Pope stated:

> For the disciples of Jesus, yesterday, today and always, the only authority is the authority of service, the only power is the power of the cross. As the Master tells us: "You know that the rulers of the Gentiles lord it over them, and their great men exercise authority over them. It shall not be so among you; but whoever would be great among you must be your servant, and whoever would be first among you must be your slave" (*Mt* 20:25-27).[21]

Archbishop Mark Coleridge of Australia wrote that this was a truly remarkable speech and concluded by saying, "But ensuring the synodality of the whole church will be impossible, [the Pope] said, if people misunderstand the church's hierarchy and see it as a structure in which some people are placed above others."[22]

Synodality as key to the Church's future

In November 2019, Pope Francis told the Vatican Congregation for the Doctrine of the Faith's International Theological Commission that synodality will be "key" for the Church in the future. He repeated one of his powerful earlier statements: "it is what the Lord expects from the Church of the third millennium." In forming the Council of Cardinals to inform and consult with him, he told them that one of their tasks would be to "find a path for coordination between synodality and the bishop of Rome."[23] Walking together is the key to Church structure and is here to stay, as far as the Pope is concerned, and the Cardinals are asked to help make it work!

Synodalization has been introduced gradually but quite rapidly, with measures that encourage every diocese to participate. It is not just a new way enabling different groups in the Church to meet and discuss matters: it is to be THE way of Church structure for the foreseeable future, in principle and in practice.

A synod on the implications and process of synodality itself had been planned for October 2022, but the plans were interrupted by the COVID-19 pandemic; it was rescheduled for October 2023. It is meant to serve as a model of synodality for the whole Church, down to the diocesan level, which therefore involves parishes. It will be interesting to watch the ongoing process of "synodalization" in the Catholic Church. Synodalization has been introduced gradually but quite rapidly, with measures that encourage every diocese to participate. It is not just a new way enabling different groups in the Church to meet and discuss matters: it is to be THE way of Church structure for the foreseeable future, in principle and in practice.

The Secretariat of the Synod

One outcome of the Second Vatican Council's decision to form the Synod of Bishops was the setting up of a specific Secretariat for that purpose. On the Vatican website, there is a full and informative description of the Council's decisions and how they have been implemented.[24] It gives the history of the Secretariat after it was initiated at Vatican II, as well as a list of General Secretaries, lists of synods and surrounding events, news about upcoming synods, and more.

In his teaching *Episcopalis Communio* (Episcopal Communion) in September 2018, Pope Francis strengthened the Synod of Bishops and emphasized yet again the principle of synodality as "a constitutive dimension of the Church" at all levels of her existence.[25] He stated that a synod is to be understood

> as a process composed of three parts: the preparatory phase, in which the consultation of the People of God on the themes indicated by the Roman Pontiff takes place; the celebratory phase, characterized by the meeting of the assembly of Bishops; and the implementation phase, in which the conclusions of the Synod, once approved by the Roman Pontiff, are accepted by the local churches.[26]

The Constitution provides for a General Secretariat that is to be a permanent institution at the service of the Synod of Bishops, directly subject to the Pope. There will be the General Secretary, the Under-Secretary assisting the General Secretary, the Ordinary Council, and possibly other established Councils. The General Secretary and the Undersecretary are appointed by the Pope and are members of the Synod Assembly.[27]

A note of great interest and cause for celebration for many of the laity, religious sisters and women in general is that, for the first time, an Under-Secretary at the Secretariat is a woman: Nathalie Becquart, a Xaverian religious sister and a highly qualified and experienced ecclesiologist, was appointed to this role, becoming the highest-ranking woman at the Vatican. This appointment shows Pope Francis's pledge to involve more women at the most senior levels at the Vatican and serves as a model and inspiration to other women, as well as to lay men.

Not only that, but in 2023, Sister Nathalie will become the first woman ever to be able to vote at the Synod of Bishops. This is noteworthy! Until this point, despite the progress in the numbers of laity attending synods, only Bishops could vote. Sister Nathalie's appointment can certainly be interpreted as reflecting the intention of Pope Francis to have the *whole* Church represented at synods, while her capacity to vote may raise the possibility of extending that capacity to other participating members of the laity in the future.

Reflection questions

1. Why do you think Pope Francis refers so often to the concept of the *whole* Church?

2. Pope Francis reminds the bishops that they are called to serve. What does he mean by that?

3. Reflect on the role lay people have in the Church in terms of "walking together." How do you walk with others? How would you like to walk together?

4. Do you think the appointment of a woman to an important position in the Church will make a difference to Church life? If so, how? If not, why not?

4

New Approaches at the Synods on Marriage and the Family (2014 and 2015)

The use of questionnaires

Some developments that led to more involvement by the local Church before synods include asking any Catholic who wishes to contribute to submit a questionnaire. Forms are sent to all the dioceses, which in turn make them available to parishes. The forms may be completed online and submitted to the parish or however each diocese arranges to forward them to Rome. Time is given for a diocese to explain to its members the reason for the forms and for parishioners to complete them, which ensures that as many people as possible can participate. In some ways, this is a simple scheme that allows for large volumes of messages and communications to be sent to the Synod Secretariat. The results are assessed and synthesized, revealing the laity's most frequently asked questions and most common concerns. We can see how this approach is an effective way of hearing people's "voices" and would offer a much broader scope for those creating the materials and working documents for synod participants.

A chance to speak, a chance to be heard

I was fortunate to be appointed an auditor at the Synod of Bishops on Marriage and the Family in 2015, which gave me the opportunity to find out what participation in a synod is like. At this synod, another major change took place: the invited laity who were attending were given the same amount of time to speak at the open sessions at the General Assembly as the bishops and dignitaries from other churches. Every representative at the synod was given exactly three minutes to make a short speech on a chosen topic relevant to the overall theme. All of us lay people were pleasantly surprised at this move. We were still somewhat in awe of the huge representation of the hierarchy at the synod who filled the vast hall, with the Pope presiding and listening to us, but all 54 lay people spoke well. We were all cautioned not to exceed the three minutes or our microphone would be muted. Most people complied…

Group discussions

Another change at this synod was that more time was given to participation in small and large groups. The whole assembly was divided into language groups, clergy and lay together. Most groups included three or four cardinals, three or four archbishops, three or four bishops, two representatives of other denominations, and six to eight lay people. A cardinal or archbishop was the leader of each group, with a relator assigned to deliver a report on the day's proceedings every evening. Work hours in Rome are usually 9:00 a.m. to 1:00 p.m. and 4:00 to 7:00 p.m. Synods meet for three full weeks, although not on weekends. The work is intensive, as you would expect when there are so many serious issues to discuss and about which to make suggestions and recommendations.

I found it a wonderful experience. I was grateful to be a representative lay person attending the six-member delegation from the Canadian Conference of Catholic Bishops and to see and hear these Canadian bishops in action at the synod. It was equally wonderful to be housed with the other international delegates in a convent on the grounds of the *Collegio Urbano*, which overlook St. Peter's Square and Basilica, with the famous dome of St. Peter's in full view of the room where we ate breakfast. Since we had so much in common as Catholic lay people striving to do the work of the synod, we made friends easily, bonding over three weeks with the other lay people in the groups we were assigned to, which remained the same over that time. In my group, the attitude of the lead bishops (an archbishop and a cardinal) was extremely inclusive and accommodating. On the whole, it was respectful and only occasionally hierarchical. This made me realize that a lay presence can be a challenge for some bishops from some cultures, although at times it seemed to be more about personal characteristics than cultural differences, as often happens when people are randomly placed together. I also realize that, as lay involvement at synods changes, there will be an adjustment period as each side learns to deal with some of the tensions that might occur. Group dynamics are group dynamics, whether clerical or lay!

> As lay involvement at synods changes, there will be an adjustment period as each side learns to deal with some of the tensions that might occur. Group dynamics are group dynamics, whether clerical or lay!

There is work involved

In my small group, I found I had plenty to say on most topics, since I teach graduate courses on the theological ethics of marriage and sexuality. Most of my input was fully discussed, absorbed and sometimes used in our daily report. The other lay participants also made substantial contributions to discussions, with knowledge gained from their involvement in ministries concerning marriage and the family. It was beneficial for everyone and of great general interest to find out how annulments or remarriage, for example, are handled in other parts of the world. When Pope Francis wrote his exhortation *Amoris Laetitia* after the synod, he incorporated much of the synod's reports. It was encouraging to recognize some of the points our groups made, although there's no doubt most of the other 23 groups made similar points, given the subject matter.

We were given quite a lot of reading material for homework, which prompted much discussion in our residence after hours and during the long afternoon break, when we found ourselves discussing points and insights and how these had been received in different groups. We were a fair mix of conservative to middle-of-the-road delegates, all working on some aspect of marriage and family in our home dioceses on every continent. Several bishops were also stationed at our residence; their views had a profound impact, reflecting the political situation in the country they represented. This helped us acquire some knowledge beyond our own small group's discussions and opinions. Occasionally, our views were quite diverse – perhaps the usual division of conservative and progressive, although those terms are inadequate.

The four-hour morning session included a coffee break; we joked about the crush and apparent lack of any "ladies first" approach when espresso is being served, but mostly we admired the way the Pope appeared along with everyone else for the break, chatting with people as he moved through the crowd. An impressive point was how readily he chatted with people as we arrived for or left the sessions. If one was anywhere near him, he could be counted on for a smile, a handshake and a few words. He certainly has charisma as well as stamina, sitting in full view at every session for three weeks (apart from papal audiences on Wednesday mornings) and not appearing to fall asleep or even yawn, as so many of us did, especially in the evening sessions.

Even later in the day, the atmosphere in the Synod Hall was nearly always exciting. What would this or that session bring? All of us loved the personal sessions, when each person had the opportunity to speak on a topic he or she had chosen, thus covering multiple issues. We evaluated each other's performance later and were sometimes amazed at our different views. It brought home to us the realization that the Catholic Church has a truly global perspective. It was humbling to discover that we knew so little about current matters touching on religion, many of which were revealed as some bishops spoke about the difficult circumstances in which they live.

What about the vote?

One thing lay people cannot do at synods is vote on the issues. At the time I was very keen to do so. I regretted that I didn't have that opportunity, considering the importance of some of the topics – such as the question of reception of the Eucharist after divorce and remarriage, which remained a source of tension throughout. A wise person pointed out that some moves to include lay people further were progressing, perhaps *piano piano*, gently, gently, but still progressing! So, patience, patience! This is true, and I had to acknowledge that much progress has been made at and through these synods, although the idea of involving the whole Church still, to me, was difficult to achieve. But, as the Pope has frequently observed in his teachings, "Time is greater than space…." The synodal process itself, once begun, is part of the gradual change.

Reflection questions

1. Did you know that lay people can attend synods in Rome and be active participants? What do you think about this opportunity?

2. What topic would you like to see discussed at a synod in Rome, in your diocese or in your parish?

3. Have you been able to answer a questionnaire that is now part of the preparatory phase of a Synod of Bishops? Why are these questionnaires important?

<u>5</u>

The International Theological Commission and Synodality

The topics raised in the International Theological Commission's document *Synodality in the Life and Mission of the Church* aim to offer a clear theological and pastoral understanding of synodality, walking together. I mainly draw on these topics for this primer.[28] It is relatively straightforward to describe the synodal process and the evolving ways of shaping actions and best practices to allow everyone's voice to be heard. Before this happens, however, theological and pastoral approaches must be set within the parameters of official teaching. In Catholic teaching, everything must be rooted in and viewed through the lenses of Scripture and Tradition. The International Theological Commission document follows that path, placing the concept of synodality amid its scriptural and theological roots – especially in the context of the Council of Jerusalem (Acts 16) and the Vatican II document *Lumen Gentium*, as discussed in previous chapters.

Rooted in Scripture and Tradition

The document begins with the biblical foundations, referencing the Council of Jerusalem and the councils and synods that have taken place over the centuries since Christianity became established, as noted earlier. It states its intention of going deeper into the theology of Vatican II, especially its ecclesiology – the theology of the Church itself – "linking them with the perspective of the pilgrim and missionary People of God and with the mystery of Church as communion."[29] Section 10 also looks at "the participation of all the members of the People of God in the mission of the Church and the exercise of authority by their pastors." It is clear that there are lessons to be learned about such participation on all fronts.

The document notes that in the more than 50 years since the last Council, "the awareness of the Church as communion has grown in broad sectors of the People of God and there have been positive experiences of synodality at diocesan, regional and universal levels."[30] Many Synods of Bishops have been held, and conferences of bishops have become more active. Various types of synodal assembly have also met to discuss national and local matters. The Commission wants to show that all sectors of the Church need to do likewise, reminding us in section 42 that the Pope has declared that "Synodality is an essential dimension of the Church."[31]

This is an important ecclesial and theological claim, based on Pope Francis's insight that it is essential in the sense that "what the Lord is asking of us is already in some sense present in the very word."[32] This emphasizes once again that synodality is not a new concept: it can be seen from the beginning of the Church in how the Apostles proceeded at the Council of Jerusalem and in synods over the centuries. It is important for us to retrieve the knowledge that the Apostles looked to the leadership of the Holy Spirit for guidance in discerning the way forward: they were mindful that Jesus himself had pointed out "the Way" to them many times and had promised the Spirit to his followers. The Church has rarely strayed completely from this approach, but variations have occurred. The question of hierarchical authority and leadership versus lay leadership has been slowly evolving. From the Enlightenment

THE INTERNATIONAL THEOLOGICAL COMMISSION AND SYNODALITY

period (17th and 18th centuries) on, democratic processes have developed, encouraging a move away from aristocratic entitlement and toward a more egalitarian right of participation. The frequently used terms "shepherd" and "sheep" in the Church do not need to mean that the laity exists only to be led; rather, they can be seen in a more positive sense as each one contributing to making up the flock, and the flock not being complete without them all.

This idea of completeness is important for walking together and for its emphasis on the whole Church. Some of the more theological points in the Commission's document highlight this, talking about such ideas as "the responsible and ordered participation of all its members in discerning and putting into practice ways of fulfilling its mission" and referring to *Gaudium et Spes* in saying, "the call to communion with others comes through sincere self-giving, union with God and unity with our brothers and sisters in Christ."[33]

Synodality is likewise brought about "through the action of the Spirit in the communion of the Body of Christ and in the missionary journey of the People of God."[34] Catholic teaching assures us that

> The gift of the Holy Spirit, which is one and the same in all who have been baptised, is manifested in many forms: the equal dignity of the baptised; the universal call to holiness; the participation of all the faithful in the priestly, prophetic and royal office of Jesus Christ; the richness of hierarchical and charismatic gifts; the life and mission of each local Church.[35]

We know this to be the basis of our faith, but we – perhaps especially the laity – need to be more intentional about incorporating it into our daily lives and accepting it as a basis for action and consultation. The Commission further notes that (then) Cardinal Ratzinger (later Pope Benedict XVI) had written in 1996: "Being truly 'synodal', therefore, means moving forward in harmony, spurred on by the Holy Spirit."[36]

While we might tend to think of synods as *events* that happen routinely now at the Vatican and even elsewhere, the Commission asks us to look further, to see that synodality offers "a specific description of the historical development of the Church as such, breathes life into her structures and directs her mission."[37] The Church's theologies of the Trinity, of Christ and of the Eucharist are the ongoing elements in the ongoing mystery of the Church in which synodality, walking together, is an always evolving practice. This reflects yet again the point Pope Francis often makes: that synodality is an essential element of the Church and has in some form or other been present in the Church since its beginning. The Church is now in the process of retrieving this principle and, as the Commission suggests, is breathing new life into it.

> In Catholic teaching, everything must be rooted in and viewed through the lenses of Scripture and Tradition. The International Theological Commission document follows that path, placing the concept of synodality amid its scriptural and theological roots — especially in the context of the Council of Jerusalem (Acts 16) and the Vatican II document Lumen Gentium.

The authority of bishops

The Commission acknowledges the authority of the bishops to discern and decide about issues, saying that "the authority of pastors is a specific gift of the Spirit of Christ the head for the upbuilding of the entire body, not a delegated and representative function of the people."[38] While the importance of consulting everyone in the Church is recognized, it must be in conformity with the decision-making capacity of the leadership by the bishops, with and under the leadership of the Pope. The Commission knew that some would say that "the Church is not a democracy" and that there could be concerns on the part of some bishops that their leadership is being challenged. Yet those concerns should not prohibit the process of synodality, where the *sensus fidei*, the need for agreement by the whole Church in matters of faith and morals, is presented as essential to the discernment of the bishops, under the guidance of the Spirit.[39] The real challenge is to keep this practice within the scope of its theological groundings, even as it is carried out in pastoral practice. The Commission reminds us of the theological underpinnings of a synodal assembly, which involve "responding to the summons of the Lord, listening as a community to what the Spirit is saying to the Church through the Word of God which resonates in their situation, and interpreting the signs of the times with the eyes of faith."[40]

Theologian John O'Malley sums up the broad scope of the Commission's document and its support for synodality in remarking:

> The report unmistakably makes church governance an open question because it advocates a change in the way church governance has generally functioned since Vatican I. It advocates the reintroduction of diocesan, regional, national and international synods as a regular feature of church life. It also reveals the ambitious scope of the proposal. It envisages synodality as operative on every level of church structure—diocesan, regional or national, and international. It explicitly states, moreover, that "the participation of the faithful is essential" at every level.[41]

O'Malley seems to share the concern of the Commission in the final chapter of its document, where it acknowledges that neither the bishops nor the laity are accustomed to this way of proceeding in the Church. The Commission implies that a change in the mentality of both will not be easy, and more likely will be a long-term project.

Not, however, if Pope Francis has a say in the matter! The new format for synods was introduced in every diocese in 2021 in preparation for the synod in 2023. Every diocese is expected to participate: this is key to having the views of the laity expressed, documented and presented to the Synod Secretariat in preparation for the next phase. This practice was done for the last three synods, and dioceses seem to have adapted well to the process.

The Commission also took note of Pope Francis's detailed speech in 2015 celebrating the 50th anniversary of the Synod of Bishops in its deliberations on the need for participation of the whole Church, beginning locally – at the diocesan level. The Pope insisted that "The first level of the exercise of *synodality* is had in the particular Churches."[42]

While the Church is well organized internally to arrange meetings and synods, the Pope reminded Church leaders that all their arrangements must "start from people and their daily problems" if a Synodal Church is to develop.[43]

One member of the sub-commission spoke to this point in an interview. He noted a growing awareness that the local Church be more represented at synods, because although synods are meant for bishops to attend, "the topics discussed at the synod are not always previously discussed with the local churches." The document strongly supports this view, not only in advocating local involvement, but also in helping the next level prepare to discuss matters that affect the local Church. The Commission's document suggests simply that this ensures that "the bishops will be able to hear from the People of God about possible topics of discussion, *before* synod assemblies" (emphasis added).

By the time the Commission's document was published in 2018, involvement at local levels was already under way through the work of the Synod Secretariat, which asked that the questionnaires their office sent to every diocese for the Synod on Marriage and the Family in 2014 be completed. In turn, each diocese had to make these available to every parish; any parishioner who chose to do so had access to the questionnaire and knew where and how to return it. This practice is to be carried out before every Synod of Bishops takes place.

Cardinal Grech, Secretary of the Synod, confirmed the importance of this first, local phase when he said: "The Second Vatican Council teaches that the People of God participate in the prophetic office of Christ. Therefore, we must listen to the People of God, and this means going out to the local churches."[44]

Reflection questions

1. What do you understand by the words "synodality is an essential dimension of the Church"?

2. Why is it important for local churches to be involved?

3. How is this involvement organized?

4. Have you found it possible to have your voice heard at the parish or diocesan level?

6

Learning from Countries with Experience of Synods

Some countries have held national or local synods, some synods are in process, and others are in the planning stages. It is encouraging to see these developments: their outcomes will be important not just locally and nationally but also globally.

Germany: A lesson on keeping the Holy Spirit at the centre of synodal assemblies

The synod arranged by the Church in Germany caused some concern externally as well as internally and became a lightning rod for some critiques of synodality that have emerged. In looking briefly at the synod's development, we can see why that is so.

In 2019, the Catholic population in Germany fell by nearly 273,000, continuing a decline that had become apparent several years before. The German bishops commissioned a study into sexual abuse in 2018. The study concluded that, over long periods of time, abuse by individual priests and religious had been shielded by power structures in the Church through secrecy and lack of transparency, as well as, for many years, a lack of knowledge of psychology, human sexuality and the likelihood of an abuser returning to abusive behaviour. Church leaders decided to hold a national synodal meeting, the *Synodaler Weg* (Synodal Way or Path), focused on power and authority in the Church and on sexuality.[45]

The bishops collaborated with a lay group, the Central Committee of German Catholics, and planned to add other stress points, such as priestly celibacy, LGBTQ+ issues and the role of women. This was all in the context of a severe crisis caused by the revelation of so many cases of sexual abuse and what appeared to be cover-ups by some bishops.

Cardinal Marx, the leader of the German Conference of Bishops when the synod began to be organized, had already made statements about abuse, women's ordination and other issues. These led some people to see the German Church as perhaps overly progressive in its positions, in both pastoral and doctrinal matters.[46] The prospect of a national assembly taking its own steps toward resolving doctrinal issues caused some concern at the Vatican, which was mindful of its global responsibilities and the effects such decisions could have in other parts of the Catholic world.

The Catholic News Agency reported that "The group is focused on four study areas: power and the separation of powers in the church; relationships and sexuality; priestly ministry, including conversations about celibacy; and women in ministries and offices in the church."[47] All contentious issues and of concern to every Catholic!

A major cause for concern was that not only did the assembly include many lay people, but they would be able to vote and therefore would have direct influence in decision making and results. This point differs from established practice at Synods of Bishops, where lay attendees do not vote. Allowing lay participants to vote raised the possibility of their synod being more democratic or even parliamentary in style, where the decision of the majority would prevail, thus challenging the authority of the bishops.

Cardinal Gerhard Müller, former prefect of the Congregation for the Doctrine of the Faith, had concerns about this approach. He made a distinction that he hoped the 2021–23 synod would underline. Synodality, he wrote, is of two different kinds: "the synodality of bishops as teachers and pastors, and the synodality of the Christian community, which can be a help to the decision-makers but must not infringe on their authority."[48] The question of the authority of the bishops is certainly a delicate one these days, but the Pope himself has stressed that it is essential. Future Church synods in Rome may include more lay people, but Catholic teaching is clear that the bishops, apostolic successors to Peter, are the authority figures in the Church, with the Pope as head. At the same time as some fears about a takeover by the laity were being expressed, one commentator said: "It is true that the synodal path is discussing changes to doctrine; however, every expert I spoke with—even one outspoken critic—reiterated that the German church has no intention of breaking from Rome or attempting to change doctrine without Rome's approval, even if none of their proposals are accepted."[49]

Pope Francis's reminder to the Church in Germany

When the proposed study areas focusing on authority and sexuality were announced in the summer of 2019, Pope Francis wrote to the German Church, warning about the temptation to "go it alone," striving independently to solve its problems, thereby possibly creating even more. The Pope reminded them that the synodal process demands a dual perspective:

> first, "bottom up," meaning from the grassroots daily experiences of the communities and people; and then "top down," which involves the collegial ministry of the bishops. "Only in this way can we reach and take decisions on questions that are essential for the faith and the life of the church."[50]

He emphasized the need for updating information in many areas where people held different opinions and welcomed input on how the German Church could move forward, recognizing that there are rarely immediate results in such matters. He reminded them that it takes time for mature results to come, for "true reform to come about through inner conversion."[51] Such conversion is a fundamental necessity for true walking together; it will need to be repeated over the years to ensure that proceedings and conclusions of synodal gatherings will be genuinely spiritual.

The central role of the Spirit

In emphasizing that evangelization must be the guiding factor, the Pope underlined the central role of the Spirit in the synodal journey. German Catholics (and everyone else) must listen to the Spirit in discerning what will make the Church "more faithful, able, agile and transparent to preach the Gospel with joy."[52] This should surely be the intention of every synodal assembly. No doubt the Pope intended this letter, which is very detailed, to be observed universally in any such gatherings.

He also emphasized the need to keep the *sensus ecclesiae* (the sense of Church) alive in all their decisions and to stay in communion with the whole body of the Church: "Let us walk together along the way, as an apostolic body, and listen to each other under the guidance of the Holy Spirit, even if we do not think the same way ... the Lord shows us the way of the Beatitudes."[53]

> In emphasizing that evangelization must be the guiding factor, the Pope underlined the central role of the Spirit in the synodal journey.

Synods are about listening, not political decisions

The General Secretariat of the Synod followed up on the Pope's reminder by issuing guidelines reminding those about to hold synods that these assemblies cannot make binding decisions for the Church. A lay representative from the German *Weg* responded that this and other concerns had already been addressed in a newer version of the planning documents, and that they had agreed to make recommendations to the Vatican at the Synod of Bishops on Synodality, recognizing that the whole Church must be involved.[54]

In his letter, the Pope clearly expressed his concerns about the possibility of a "wrong" path:

> At times, I feel a great sadness when I see a community that, with good will, takes a wrong path because it thinks it is making the church through gatherings, as if it were a political party: the majority, the minority, what this one thinks of this or that or the other.... *I ask myself: "Where is the Holy Spirit there? Where is prayer? Where is communitarian love? Where is the Eucharist?"* Without these four coordinates, the church becomes a human society, a political party.[55] (emphasis added)

The Pope's letter was effective: in June 2021, he met with the new president of the German bishops' conference, accepting and encouraging the "way" presented to him with questionable aspects removed or improved. The Pope was not saying that, for example, talking about changes in doctrine should not occur; he did not forbid anything, but he was clear that any conclusions would not be binding on the German Church. Instead, they would be submitted for possible discussion at the next Synod of Bishops. The Pope was crystal clear about the essence of synodality, speaking at an audience with a delegation from Italian Catholic Action: "There cannot be synodality without the Spirit, and there is no Spirit without prayer."[56]

Pope Francis's teaching is clear: synods of all types must follow this prayerful approach, guided procedurally by the Office of the Synod. In that way, even questions of doctrinal change can be raised, discussed and voted upon as recommendations. This is important for synodal assemblies at all levels, since doors are not closed on some proposals at early stages: in the true spirit of synod, even controversial matters might be discussed and perhaps recommended for further discussion. Recommendations from local synods which deal with pastoral matters will be referred to the local bishop and most likely an appointed synod committee to discern how to implement the changes suggested.

Archdiocese of Liverpool diocesan synod: A model for dialogue on pastoral issues at the diocesan level

An example of a local pastoral synod was the one organized by the Archdiocese of Liverpool, England, in 2020–2021, concluding with several pastoral recommendations to be forwarded to the archbishop and his committee of evaluation.[57] The agenda was quite different from that of the German conference, given that this was a diocesan synod and more limited in scope, discussing pastoral rather than doctrinal matters. While not dealing with controversial points of doctrine, this type of synod models a way for a diocese to come together to discover what the whole local Church would like to see happen pastorally and to make decisions about priorities. The Liverpool synod is well documented, with a useful website listing its events and webinars, and joyful lay participation was evident.

A review of its 19 recommendations and the voting patterns shows that some suggestions may be globally as well as locally representative of the state of the Church. For example, training and teaching about sacraments in parishes for adults was not high on the participants' list of priorities. Better education about the sacraments for high school students ranked much higher, suggesting that participants were more concerned about young people's knowledge than about their own. This type of recommendation indicates a common perceived need, where a diocese could then concentrate its efforts.

The Archdiocese consulted the Office of the Synod at the Vatican before the local synod began, and Sister Nathalie Bequart, Under-Secretary of the Office of the Synod, followed up in a webinar with the synodal leaders in Liverpool, further explaining procedure and encouraging them on their synodal way.[58] She explained, using a process sheet, how Liverpool's synod would contribute to the Synod on Synodality in 2023. Every diocese will follow the same steps and, although topics for discussion will differ, there will be similarities. The results will be categorized and organized at the Synod Office and presented to the Synod of Bishops on Synodality in 2023 as its working document, or *Instrumentum Laboris*.[59]

Ireland: National synodal assembly

Ireland's Catholic bishops announced in March 2021 that they would hold a national synodal assembly within the next five years, noting that it was more than timely, since secularization, clerical abuse and the Irish mother-and-baby homes scandals[60] necessitated a national discussion where all voices could be heard. The synodal assembly was to begin with two years of prayer, listening, consultation and discernment and would include a consultative dialogue on national matters as well as on the meaning of synodality. Although partly designed to encourage and aid the Irish Church's participation in the Synod of Bishops that will conclude in 2023, it was mostly seen as a way to allow people to express their anger and grief over abuse issues as well as to address ways to build trust and move forward.

Australia: Plenary council and the *sensus fidei*

Australia has also planned a national assembly, a plenary council, which, according to its website, will make decisions about pastoral matters; those "made at the council become binding for the Catholic Church in Australia."[61] The Australian bishops said this is needed since contemporary society has changed significantly, and the Royal Commission into Institutional Responses to Child Sexual Abuse necessitated deep reflection and discussion on how to respond appropriately. They, like Pope Francis, emphasize the *sensus fidei*, the agreement of the whole Church, in an insightful statement:

No individual has an infallible sense of the faith. We only have a sense of what God is wanting by allowing as many as possible to have a voice in the conversation God wants to have with the church. Singly we see a special viewpoint; together we see much more.[62]

They also made an important teaching point: the need to discern and listen to the Spirit is the same instruction that was given to the seven churches of Asia Minor in the Book of Revelation. Vatican II talked of how God, who spoke in the past, "continues to converse" with the Church (*Dei Verbum*, no. 8); now the Church in Australia "hopes to enter more intensely into that divine-human dialogue."[63]

These types of approaches might help encourage all national and local Churches to be even more involved in synodal gatherings, as well as responding to questions from the Secretariat of the Synod from Rome. Such involvement is even more likely to happen if it is known, as it was in the German example, that topics that are thought possibly dangerous and unwelcome may be raised and discussed without prejudice to the Church's stand on them, since nothing binding in matters of doctrine may be decided at a local or national level. If synods have a purpose, it is surely to allow questions to be raised and answered in some form.

Reflection questions

1. What can we learn from the way the German Church organized its synodal path?

2. What sorts of issues do you think synods could discuss?

3. Would a local diocesan or parish synod help your local Church in some way? How?

4. Do you think most parishioners feel they have a voice in the Church? Do you? Why?

7

Synodality:
From Event to Process

The Synod of Bishops on Synodality was originally planned for October 2021 but was rescheduled because of the COVID-19 pandemic. The pandemic also delayed some national and diocesan synods. The Secretary of the Synod, Cardinal Grech, said that these delays gave the Secretariat the opportunity to comply with the arrangements set out in the Pope's teaching in *Episcopalis Communio* (Episcopal Communion).[64] As mentioned earlier, Pope Francis published this important document in September 2018, shedding new light on the purpose of synods. Before that, a synod was viewed more as an ecclesial event that opened and closed in a fixed time, usually about three to four weeks, and was attended by elected bishops along with other representatives.

In re-establishing the importance of the Synod of Bishops, Pope Paul VI had stated that part of their purpose was "to facilitate discussion, at least on the essential points of doctrine and on the course of action to be taken in the life of the Church."[65] Cardinal Grech referred to the work of Pope Paul VI in an interview discussing developments in the organization of synods.[66] He also made an insightful statement that sums up the changes made during the papacy of Francis: "The first and greatest innovation is the transformation of the Synod from an event into a process": now every synod will consist of three successive phases: preparation, celebration and implementation.[67]

The first phase: Preparation / consultation

The first phase consults the People of God in their home dioceses, in accordance with Pope Francis's reminder that the Church must pay attention to the *sensus fidei*, the inerrancy of the whole Church in considering faith and morals, which Cardinal Grech sees as one of the Pope's strongest themes. The Church's self-understanding as the People of God reflects traditional teaching and, as we saw earlier in referring to *Lumen Gentium*, this *sensus fidei* ensures that "The entire body of the faithful, anointed as they are by the Holy One, cannot err in matters of belief" (no. 12). Therefore, the whole Body, the whole People of God, must be consulted on important matters when required. Modern maxims that make sense to many people, such as "Nothing about us without us," are long preceded by the Church's maxim "That which touches upon all must be approved by all." This ancient wisdom still applies in the present day, and the People of God can surely appreciate its authenticity.

The second phase: Listening / discernment

Cardinal Grech insists that the preparatory phase is vital for the synodal process, while the second phase, discernment by local bishops, will depend on focused listening to what the People of God request. This mutual listening is very important, as it reflects the interaction between the laity and their pastors in the material presented to the Office of the Synod to be included in the working documents for synod participants. Some questions have already been raised about the weight of bishops' authority in this part of the process, but the synodal process expects that mutual listening, followed by episcopal discernment, should lead to genuine representation of lay participation in the first stage.

The third phase: Voting / implementation

Discernment by the bishops culminates in the full Synodal Assembly in the third phase, which includes representatives of other episcopal conferences, Patriarchs of the Eastern Churches and invited guests. Assuming the procedure is followed properly, Cardinal Grech looks forward to successful results, asking:

> How can we not hope for great fruits from such a broad and participatory synodal journey? Moreover, how can we not hope that the indications that emerged from the Synod will become, through the third phase, that of implementation, a vehicle of renewal and reform of the Church?[68]

In this context, and looking back to the Second Vatican Council, Cardinal Grech also reminds us, perhaps the questioning laity especially, that in the second phase of synodal preparation,

> the moment of discernment is entrusted above all to those bishops who are gathered in the assembly. Some may say that this is clericalism, which is the desire to keep the Church in positions of power. However, we must not forget at least two things. The first, continually reiterated by the Pope, a synodal assembly is not a parliament.[69]

The second point the Council made is that bishops are endowed with the function of discernment through their office. This is a necessary function because of the ministry they carry out for the good of the Church. Cardinal Grech observed of the first and second phases that the merit of the process will emerge in the reciprocity between consultation and discernment. On a prudent note, he added, "However, we cannot know everything straight away; the more we walk, the more we learn as we go along. I am convinced that the experience of the next Synod will teach us much about synodality and how to implement it."[70] One step at a time!

The decision-making process in the Church should begin with listening

Still, in his speech recognizing the 50th anniversary of the institution of the Synod of Bishops at the Second Vatican Council, the Pope took pains to remind the whole Church of the necessity for consultation and the importance of the whole Church being heard properly:

> *Synodality, walking together, transcends any false ideas that it means power, rights, majority rule and so on.*

I repeat, consultation is already part of the synodal process, it constitutes its first and indispensable act. Discernment depends upon this consultation. Whoever says that it is not relevant, that it is simply a preparatory act, probably does not understand very well the importance of the *sensus fidei* of the People of God. As I have observed, in the ancient Church this was the only instance of infallibility recognized in the Church, "the entire body of the faithful … cannot err in matters of belief." Here all have their place and the opportunity to express themselves. The desire of the General Secretariat is to allow everyone to make his or her voice heard, that listening is the true 'pastoral conversion' of the Church. God willing, one of the fruits of the Synod is that we might all understand that a decision-making process in the Church always begins with listening, because only in this way can we understand how and where the Spirit wants to lead the Church.[71]

This expression of synodality may seem somewhat revolutionary, but in fact is a retrieval or restoration of the Tradition coming down to us from the early Church, from the Acts of the Apostles. We should remember that, yet again, the institutional Church has performed a type of self-analysis and has come forward with a different approach to being Church as the whole People of God.

It began this process at the Second Vatican Council, launching what Pope John XXIII hailed as an *aggiornamento* – a complete updating or modernizing of the Church – that rearranged not only its structure as an institution but also our attitude to each other as full members of the Body of Christ. The Council, after much theological discussion, discerned and interpreted "the signs of the times" through prayerful listening to the Spirit. This approach is clearly visible in the development of synodality, walking together as members of the Body of Christ.

What synodality is not

It should be emphasized that neither the Pope nor the bishops see this development or evolution as a matter of rights, and the laity must reflect on this aspect over time. It is not intended as a reallocation of power by the hierarchy, or as a struggle for equal rights for the laity in a legalistic, political way. If it is seen as the movement of the Spirit, invoked as guide and interpreted by those whose prayerful collaboration at the Second Vatican Council led to the recognition (literally, a "re-cognition") of the Church as the People of God, then we will be able to accept these changes as the "way" in which the Spirit beckons.

The Church has never been and should not be labelled a democracy, but, theologically speaking, every member has a role to play and a voice to be heard conferred by baptism. The responsibility of Church leadership is to discern issues in light of those voices, guided by the Spirit. In this vein, synodality, walking together, transcends any false ideas that it means power, rights, majority rule and so on.

We cannot afford to be naïve: the temptations associated with power are universal and timeless, but so are the God-given powers of critique, analysis and paying attention, allied with faith, hope and trust in Jesus Christ and the Spirit he bequeathed us. What other body on earth takes this global approach, time travelling back to the Council of Jerusalem: the leaders gather with the people; the people, with tales to tell and questions about practices to resolve, tell these publicly; and the leaders pronounce judgment – all guided by the Spirit? If there is a better "way," the same Spirit will lead us to discover it. Right now, the discernment of the Church at and since the Second Vatican Council and since Pope Paul's founding of the Synod of Bishops has resulted in synodality – a process, not an event, modelled closely on that first, successful Council in the new Christian era.

Reflection questions

1. Why is there emphasis on synod as process?

2. Can you describe the various stages that the process takes?

3. Does any point about how synods are to be structured inspire you or confuse you?

4. Reflect on the changes made to involve the laity in synods, together with clergy. How do these changes affect how you see your role as a member of the Church?

Conclusion

The theme of the Synod on synodality in 2023 is "For a Synodal Church: Communion, Participation and Mission." Theology today talks increasingly about mission, which is a fundamental characteristic of Christianity. Religion and spirituality are not meant to be only personally beneficial, although they often are: the "going forth" element is what makes us evangelizers. Inward spiritual nourishment is essential for giving and sharing with others, but at the end of every celebration of the Eucharist, we are enjoined to "go!" "Go! You are sent forth!" It is a command, although some variations of the command are gentler. As members of the Body of Christ, we are called to promote that Body internally and externally by sharing our lives with our fellow members but also by reaching out to encourage more people to become members or to strengthen their existing membership. The International Theological Commission writes that this is also true of synodality:

> Synodality is lived out in the Church in the service of mission…. The whole People of God is an agent of the proclamation of the Gospel. Every baptised person is called to be a protagonist of mission since we are all missionary disciples. The Church is called, in synodal synergy, to activate the ministries and charisms present in her life and to listen to the voice of the Spirit, in order to discern the ways of evangelisation.[72]

Go, you are sent forth!

Afterword:
A Personal Note

Because I attended the Synod on Marriage and the Family in 2015, I became even more interested in the concept of synodality that we were discussing at International Theological Commission meetings. I was especially interested in the implications for change in the role of the laity. The role of bishops is clearer, but what difference would changes in the role of laity mean? The re-emphasis on the need for dioceses to update their practice by having synods at different levels is important, following Vatican II's recommendation of establishing pastoral councils, which still may be non-existent or inactive in some dioceses and parishes. Yet creating and maintaining these councils is fundamental to practising synodality, as it fosters greater lay participation and involvement.

When questions were asked about lay involvement in synods, I was able to explain that, from my limited experience of attending one synod, lay people added a lot to the discussions. I agreed that as a theologian I was better informed than many about the theological aspects of sexual ethics and family life, but pastoral insights are gained as much, if not more so, from experience as from education alone. I found most of my lay colleagues well suited to provide information from the grassroots through working with people dealing with problems that sometimes run counter to official Church teaching.

Divorce and remarriage and questions of reception of the Eucharist were perhaps the hottest topics of the synod; as I told the Commission, I realized afterwards that in some way I had hoped the synod would solve these questions. It did not, and this is not surprising, since the doctrinal and canonical aspects are so important and so long-standing that, even with a noticeable shift to a more merciful approach in certain situations, these questions are far from being agreed upon by a consensus and therefore are not ready to be changed, if they ever are. Synodality itself, however, allowed these discussions to take place openly, including the views of laity, some of whom spoke to these particular questions in their allotted three-minute speech.

I discussed the point that the numbers of lay people invited to attend synods has been increasing, that participating and not just observing is expected, that contributions had been made at various levels, and that in general, laity played a significant role in the whole process. Also, I said that it was exciting to read *Amoris Laetitia* after the synod and to recognize some of the contributions of one's own group, or even one's own contributions, at certain points in the encyclical.

More controversially, I added that the Commission's document could suggest that lay people should be allowed to vote at Synods of Bishops on synodal recommendations, since lay people contribute to forming these recommendations together with the bishops. This was not received well. Cardinal Müller, who was the Chair of the Commission, did not express an opinion on this issue at the time. On the whole, he did not say much or intervene at the meetings, but allowed the members to speak for themselves. The suggestion did not garner much support from the whole group, or from the sub-commission drafting the document, which sent an envoy later to ask why I was putting that view forward. Didn't I know it was a Synod of Bishops, with emphasis on "bishops"? Yes, of course I knew that, but since part of the discussion about synodality is about lay participation and contribution, then if lay people actually do participate and contribute and that is welcomed and accepted, it seemed reasonable to me that we should also vote on proposals at voting time. I was well aware that not everyone thought that way, but, after all, here I was at an International Theological Commission meeting discussing synodality as the "way" forward together. It was the perfect opportunity to speak up, as the Commission itself was "walking together," mostly very well! No one else shared my view on voting, and it was not mentioned in the final document. Perhaps it was too political, and I realize it could have upset the balanced view of synodality the Commission was striving to establish for general acceptance in the Church.

I should add that I made it clear that I did not mean my proposal as a political statement on the rights of the laity. Rather, I see it as a natural outcome of the concept of synodality, if "walking together" is to be taken seriously. In no way was the proposal meant to challenge the authority of the bishops or their collegial role in exercising that authority.

I repeat: it's not a matter of equal rights. Those are about law and discrimination, and law is always secondary to faith, morals and the cardinal virtues, the first of which is prudence! But then the second cardinal virtue is justice, which is not unimportant here. I fully appreciate that decision making lies in the authority of the role of bishops, and I agree with that Spirit-given authority. I am talking only about voting at *synods* in line with what we as lay people voiced, and not suggesting we be part of the decision making in our individual dioceses in the ongoing business of governance and procedure there. I think there is a difference, but as yet, that thinking is unsupported.

A promising sign

Nonetheless, the appointment in 2020 of Sister Nathalie Bequart as the first female Under-Secretary at the Secretariat of the Synod means that a woman, technically a lay person (religious women are lay people), *will* be able to vote at the next synod, for the first time!

Once that has been witnessed and recorded, then perhaps other possibilities may be accepted. Sister Nathalie is careful to point out that her appointment is not about women's rights. Rather, it reflects the meaning of synodality: working together, discerning together and, in her case, participating in reaching conclusions about further actions and in voting with the bishops on them. I suggest that it's all connected.

As the Commission continued to work on the draft document, I did not raise another suggestion going through my mind: that there be equal numbers of clerics and lay people at synodal assemblies, even Synods of Bishops. It would have been imprudent at that point, especially since my first point sank like a stone. This other point will have to wait for another person to suggest it at another time, perhaps when synodality is established in a more fully fledged way and is reviewed, some time from now, to see how effective it is and what could be added or omitted.

Notes

1   Anne Louise Mahoney, ed., *Looking to the Laity: Reflections on Where the Church Can Go from Here* (Toronto: Novalis, 2021), 128.
2   Papal Basilica of St Paul Outside-the-Walls website, "The Council of Jerusalem," https://www.vatican.va/various/basiliche/san_paolo/en/san_paolo/concilio.htm.
3   Jaroslav Pelikan, *Acts. Brazos Commentary on the Bible* (Brazos Press, 2003).
4   Ibid.
5   Ibid.
6   Second Vatican Council, *Lumen Gentium,* Dogmatic Constitution on the Church (1964), vatican.va.
7   Paul Lakeland, *A Council that Will Never End: Lumen Gentium and the Church Today* (Liturgical Press, 2013), 84.
8   Massimo Faggioli, *A Council for a Global Church: Receiving Vatican II in History* (Fortress Press, 2015), 241.
9   Ibid., 232, 233.
10 "Synodality, collegiality: Two keys to the coming Francis reform," Catholic Voices website (August 28, 2013), https://cvcomment.org/2013/08/28/synodality-collegiality-two-keys-to-the-coming-francis-reform.
11 Ibid.
12 Ibid.
13 Pope Francis, Apostolic Exhortation *Evangelii Gaudium: The Joy of the Gospel,* November 24, 2013, vatican.va.
14 Pope Francis, "Address," Ceremony Commemorating the 50th Anniversary of the Institution of the Synod of Bishops (October 17, 2015), https://www.vatican.va/content/francesco/en/speeches/2015/october/documents/papa-francesco_20151017_50-anniversario-sinodo.html.
15 Ibid.
16 Ibid.
17 Ibid.
18 Ibid.
19 Ibid.
20 Ibid.
21 Ibid.
22 Archbishop Mark Coleridge, "On the Road Together – The Pope's Remarkable Speech" (October 17, 2016), https://catholic.org.au/blogs/on-the-road-together-the-pope-s-remarkable-speech.
23 Ibid.
24 Secretariat of the Synod website, http://www.synod.va/content/synod/en.html.
25 Pope Francis, Apostolic Constitution *Episcopalis Communio* (September 15, 2018), vatican.va.
26 Ibid.
27 Ibid.
28 International Theological Commission, *Synodality in the Life and Mission of the Church* (Vatican, 2018), https://www.vatican.va/roman_curia/congregations/cfaith/cti_documents/rc_cti_20180302_sinodalita_en.html.
29 Ibid., no. 10.
30 Ibid.
31 Ibid., no. 42.
32 Pope Francis, "Address," Ceremony Commemorating the 50th Anniversary of the Institution of the Synod of Bishops.
33 International Theological Commission, *Synodality in the Life and Mission of the Church,* no. 47.
34 Ibid.
35 Ibid.
36 Ibid., no. 5.

37   Ibid.

38   Ibid., no. 67.

39   Second Vatican Council, *Lumen Gentium,* no. 12: "'The entire body of the faithful, anointed as they are by the Holy One, cannot err in matters of belief. They manifest this special property by means of the whole peoples' supernatural discernment in matters of faith when 'from the Bishops down to the last of the lay faithful' they show universal agreement in matters of faith and morals."

40   International Theological Commission, *Synodality in the Life and Mission of the Church*, no. 68.

41   John W. O'Malley, "Who Governs the Catholic Church? It's an Open Question," *America* (October 16, 2020).

42   Pope Francis, "Address," Ceremony Commemorating the 50th Anniversary of the Institution of the Synod of Bishops.

43   Ibid.

44   Andrea Tornielli, "Cardinal Grech: Transformation of Synod to Create Space for People of God," *Vatican News* (May 21, 2021), https://www.vaticannews.va/en/vatican-city/news/2021-05/cardinal-grech-interview-synod-secretariat-changes.html.

45   Colleen Dulle, "The German Synodal Way, Explained," *America* (June 24, 2021), https://www.americamagazine.org/faith/2021/06/24/german-synodal-path-way-explainer-240919; CNA Staff, "The German Synodal Way: A CNA Explainer," CAN website (June 14, 2021), https://www.catholicnewsagency.com/news/247992/the-german-synodal-way-a-cna-explainer.

46   Better Church Governance website, "Rheinhard Cardinal Marx," https://betterchurchgovernance.org/cardinal-marx. Current matters that would be discussed include the celibacy of the priesthood, women's ordination to the priesthood and the diaconate. This process has been rejected by both Pope Francis and the Congregation for the Clergy.

47   CNA Staff, "The German Synodal Way."

48   Cardinal Mueller, quoted in Russell Shaw, "Concerning 'Synodality" (February 10, 2021), https://www.thecatholicthing.org/2021/02/10/concerning-synodality.

49   Colleen Dulle, quoted in Mike Lewis, "German Schism vs US Schism: Competing Narratives," Where Peter Is website (June 24, 2021), https://wherepeteris.com/german-schism-vs-us-schism-competing-narratives.

50   Ibid.

51   Ibid.

52   Ibid.

53   Ibid.

54   CNA, "Bishop Batzing Says... Pope Francis Encourages Us to Continue on 'Synodal Way'" (June 29, 2021), https://thewandererpress.com/catholic/news/featured-today/bishop-batzing-says-pope-francis-encourages-us-to-continue-on-synodal-way.

55   Pope Francis, "Letter to the German Church" (June 29, 2021), https://www.vaticannews.va/en/pope/news/2019-06/pope-francis-letter-german-church-synodality.html.

56   Adélaide Patrignani, "Sister Becquart: There Is No Synodality without Spirituality" (July 26, 2021), https://www.catholicsabah.com/sister-becquart-there-is-no-synodality-without-spirituality.

57   Liverpool Synod 2020, "Highlights of Our Synod Day" (June 19, 2021), https://youtu.be/IvNA_oqxyTs.

58   "A Meeting with Sr Nathalie Bequart," webinar with Liverpool Synod representatives (June 9, 2021), https://youtu.be/nTKusJ-SYgA.

59   See the infographic on this web page: "Vatican Asks All Catholic Dioceses to Take Part in Synod on Synodality," *National Catholic Register* (May 21, 2021), https://www.ncregister.com/news/vatican-asks-all-catholic-dioceses-to-take-part-in-synod-on-synodality.

60   Government of Ireland, *Mother and Baby Homes Commission of Investigation Report* (February 2021), https://www.gov.ie/en/publication/d4b3d-final-report-of-the-commission-of-investigation-into-mother-and-baby-homes/?referrer=http://www.gov.ie/report. The report was on the abuse, deaths and unmarked graves of babies and mothers at several homes for pregnant women run by religious orders in Ireland from 1922 to 1998.

61 Australian Plenary Council, "Frequently Asked Questions," https://plenarycouncil.catholic.org.au/frequently-asked-questions.

62 Ibid.

63 Ibid.

64 Tornielli, "Cardinal Grech: Transformation of Synod to Create Space for People of God."

65 Pope Paul VI, *Motu Proprio Apostolica Sollicitudo* (September 15, 1965), vatican.va.

66 Tornielli, "Cardinal Grech: Transformation of Synod to Create Space for People of God."

67 Ibid.

68 Ibid.

69 Ibid.

70 Ibid.

71 Pope Francis, "Address," Ceremony Commemorating the 50th Anniversary of the Institution of the Synod of Bishops.

72 Ibid.